1 CORINTHIANS 13

Coloring and Activity book

iCHARACTER

www.icharacter.org
Published by iCharacter Ltd. (Ireland)
By Agnes de Bezenac
Illustrated by Agnes de Bezenac
Copyright. All rights reserved.
All Bible verses adapted from the KJV.

Copyright 2014 iCharacter Ltd. All rights reserved. No part of this book may be reproduced in any form or by any electronic or mechanical means, including information storage and retrieval systems, without written permission from the publisher or author, except in the case of a reviewer, who may quote brief passages embodied in critical articles or in a review.

If I spoke every language in the world and could sing like an angel, but I wasn't loving …

Which row follows this pattern?

①

②

③

④

"Though I speak with the tongues of men and of angels, and have not charity ..."

... Then no one would want to listen to me.

Match these shapes to the picture on the left.

"I am become as sounding brass, or a tinkling cymbal."

If I was very smart, understood everything and knew God's secret plans;

Draw what you are the best at in school.

"And though I have the gift of prophecy, and understand all mysteries, and all knowledge;"

And if I had so much faith, that I could do what is impossible;

Climb the mountain maze.

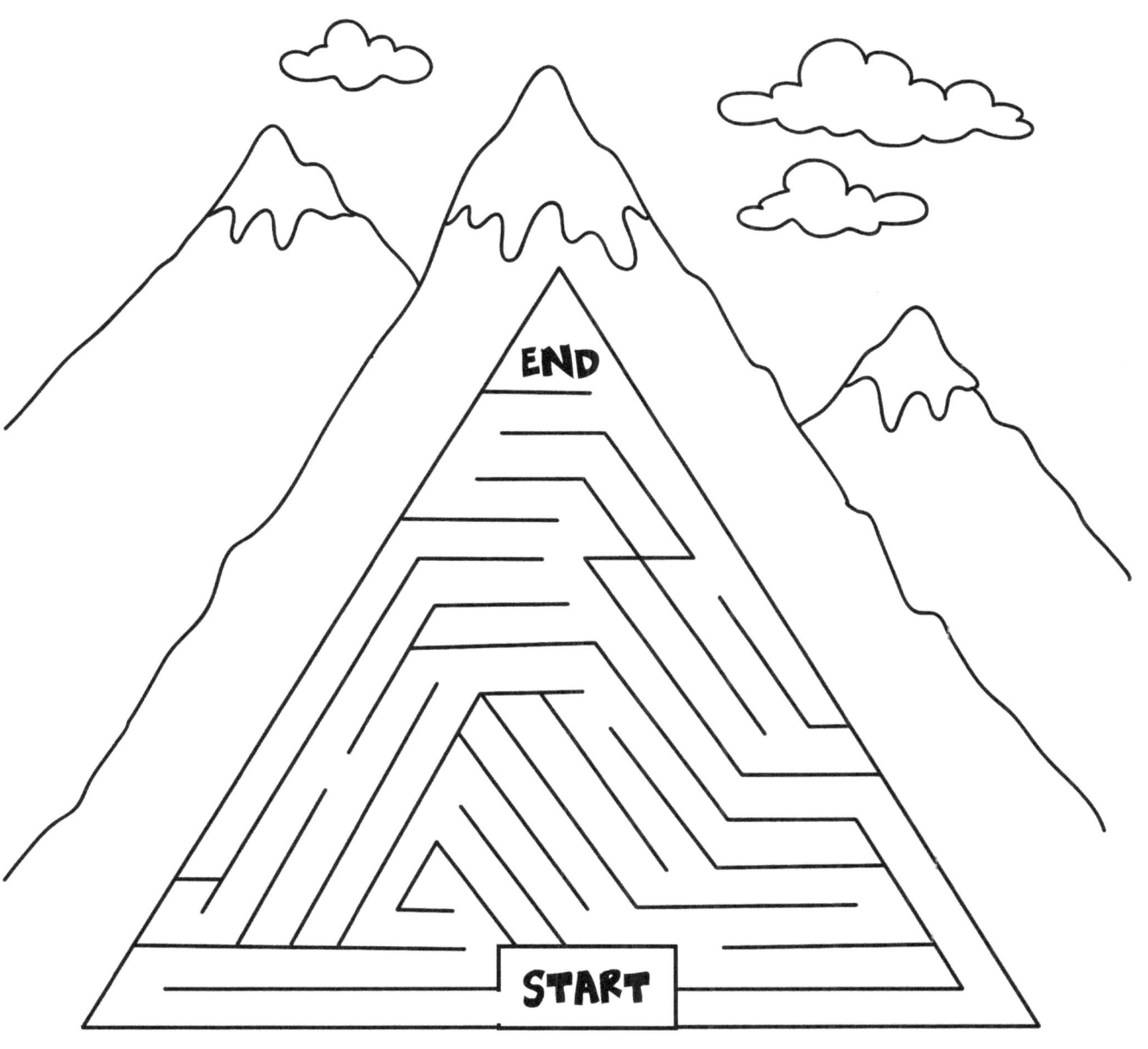

"And though I have all faith, so that I could remove mountains,"

But if I didn't love others, it would mean nothing.

How many different kinds of flowers do you see?

9   10   11   12   13

"And have not charity, I am nothing."

If I share all of my things with others, but I don't do it with love, it does me no good.

What is something that you gave away to someone who needed it more than you? Draw it in the box.

"And though I bestow all my goods to feed the poor... and have not charity, it profiteth me nothing."

Love is being patient and full of kindness.

Circle all the things that might be in a first aid kit.

"Charity suffereth long, and is kind;"

Love does not brag about what it has. When I love, I don't think of myself as better than others.

find the one that is different, in each row.

"Charity envieth not; charity vaunteth not itself, is not puffed up,"

Love is not rude, even when others are. When I'm loving, I don't always have to be first.

Match the sea shells with their shadows.

"Doth not behave itself unseemly, seeketh not her own,"

Love doesn't easily get angry,
and it doesn't remember the bad
things others do.

Draw about a time that you didn't get angry over something bad that happened to you.

"Is not easily provoked, thinketh no evil;"

Love does not enjoy bad things,
but is happy for the good.

Find your way to the happy face.

"Rejoiceth not in iniquity, but rejoiceth in the truth;"

Love takes care of others. It accepts others. Love keeps on going, even when things get difficult.

Find the six differences.

"Beareth all things, believeth all things, hopeth all things, endureth all things."

Love always works; it never gives up.

Match the caps to the balls.

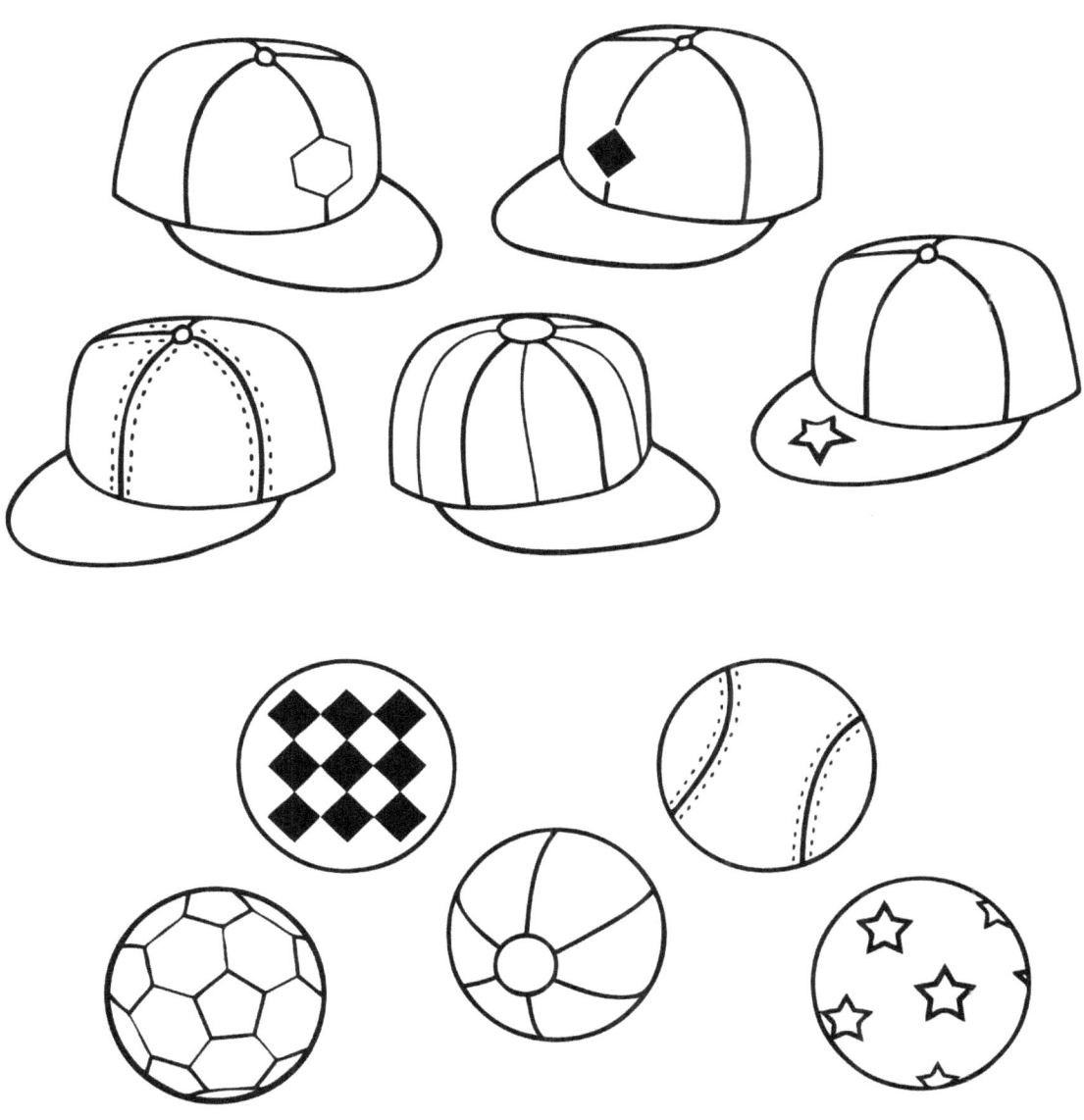

"Charity never faileth:"

I could be the smartest kid around. But it's more important to always be loving.

Color the books that might help teach you about being kind.

"But whether there be prophecies, they shall fail; whether there be tongues, they shall cease; whether there be knowledge, it shall vanish away."

There are three things that will last forever: faith, hope and love. But the most important one is love.

Find your way through the hearts by following this shape.

START

"And now abideth faith, hope, charity, these three; but the greatest of these is charity."

More books from iCharacter.org

www.ingramcontent.com/pod-product-compliance
Lightning Source LLC
Chambersburg PA
CBHW081432070526
44586CB00020B/2564